Water

Hilary Devonshire

FRANKLIN WATTS

New York/London/Toronto/Sydney

© Franklin Watts 1991

Franklin Watts, Inc.
387 Park Avenue South
New York, NY 10016

Series Editor: Hazel Poole
Editor: Jenny Wood
Design: K and Co
Artwork: Aziz Khan
Photography: Chris Fairclough; Eye Ubiquitous/Judyth Platt (p5)
Consultants: Henry Pluckrose,
Barbara Taylor, Lillian Wright

Library of Congress Cataloging-in-Publication Data

Devonshire, Hilary.
    Water / Hilary Devonshire.
       p.   cm. — (Science through art)
    Includes bibliographical references and index.
    Summary Defines and demonstrates the properties of water through
artistic experiments and projects.
    ISBN 0-531-14125-X
    1. Water—Juvenile literature.   2. Water—Experiments—Juvenile
literature.   [1. Water—Experiments.   2. Experiments.]   I. Title.
II. Series.
GB662.3.D48   1991
553.7′078—dc20   91-8376
                                                                   CIP AC

Typeset by Lineage, Watford

Printed in the United Kingdom

CONTENTS

EQUIPMENT AND MATERIALS

This book describes activities which use the following:

Aluminum foil
Board (cutting board)
Bowl
Cardboard (thin)
Cold water dyes
Cooking oil
Craft knife
Diffuser spray
Drinking straws
Dropper
Felt-tip pens (water-based)
Glue (white)
Ink – India
    – marbling inks in various colors
    – various colored inks
Jar with screw-top lid
Jelly jars
Light scope
Linseed oil
Liquid detergent
Magnifying glass
Modeling clay
Newspaper
Paint – oil
    – powder
    – water color

Paintbrushes
Paper – black paper
    – blotting paper
    – coffee filter paper
    – construction paper
    – tissue paper
    – white paper for drawing on
Paper napkins (white dinner)
Paper towels
Pen
Pencil
Ruler (metal)
Salt
Scissors
Spoon
Stapler
Stick
Thread
Tray
Water

INTRODUCTION

Water covers over 70% of the earth's surface and is probably the world's most useful substance. Every living thing needs water in order to survive.

Water is interesting because it is a liquid. It is colorless, odorless and tasteless.

By following the investigations in this book, you will learn something about the science of water and also about the nature of liquids. At the start of each section there are some scientific ideas to be explored. A scientist looks at ideas and tries to discover if they are always true, and will also investigate to see if they can be disproved. You will be working like a scientist. A scientist is curious and wants to find out about the world in which we live. A scientist tests ideas, makes investigations and experiments, and tries to explain what has happened. Your results may be surprising or unexpected, and you may find that you will need to make a new investigation or test a new idea.

You will also be an artist. You will be using water in the art activities that are included in each section. Through working with both water and the various art materials and techniques, you will make discoveries about how water behaves and how water can be used. Your finished pieces of art will be a record of your scientific findings.

WATER FLOWS

Water always flows downward, because of an invisible force called gravity. Gravity pulls everything toward the center of the earth. When water cannot go down any further, it settles at the lowest level it can find. If the surface on which it settles is completely flat, the water will not flow.

Water will not flow if it settles on a completely flat surface.

Gravity makes water flow downward.

If a drop of water falls on a flat surface, it will not flow on its own.

Water can be made to move if it is blown on or pushed.

Watch rainwater flowing in the gutter. Which way does it flow? Where else can you see water flow?

Crumpled paper art

You will need: several sheets of paper, bowls or jars of water, colored inks, a dropper and a straw.

1 Crumple a sheet of paper, then unfold it so that it makes a paper "bowl." The creases in the paper are the channels down which the water will flow. Color the water in one of the bowls or jars by adding a few drops of ink. This will allow you to see the flowing water clearly.

2 Fold in a rim about 2.5 cm (1 in) wide around the top edge of your paper "bowl."

3 Fill a dropper or straw with some of the colored water, then release a few drops around your paper bowl. Drop the water close to the rim, on the inside of the bowl. Watch where the water flows.

4 Once the water has reached the lowest parts of the channels, it may settle in small pools at the bottom. You can make a channel on the rim to pour away the extra water. Leave the paper to dry.

5 You can mount your crumpled picture on cardboard...

6 ... or you can iron out the creases with a warm iron. Notice how the colored water creates an interesting pattern in the channels.

Smudge Print

You will need: a sheet of paper, colored inks, a dropper or a straw.

1 Fold a sheet of paper in half, then open it out. Drop a few drops of different colored inks along the fold. You need only one or two drops of each color. How can you make the ink move?

2 Fold the paper in half again. With one finger, and working from the fold out towards the edges of the paper, gently press the surface. What happens to the ink? Unfold the paper and look at your finished design. It is symmetrical – one side is exactly the same as the other.

Water on a flat surface

You will need: paper, colored inks, a dropper and a straw.

1 Release one drop of colored water onto another sheet of paper, then blow gently through the straw onto the water drop. What is making the water move outward? Make another design using several different colors of ink.

WATER IS WET

Water can make dry things wet. Objects can be made damp or wet by dipping them in water. Water can be added to substances such as dry powder color to form a solution. The water acts as a solvent for the other substance.

Dry powder and water mix to form a solution.

Objects when dipped in or covered with water become damp or wet.

When you have a bath or shower you get wet all over. What does it feel like when you walk in the rain?

Wet and Dry

You will need: water, powder paint, paper, paintbrushes.

1 Mix some dry powder color with water to make wet paint.

2 Sprinkle dry powder color onto wet paper.

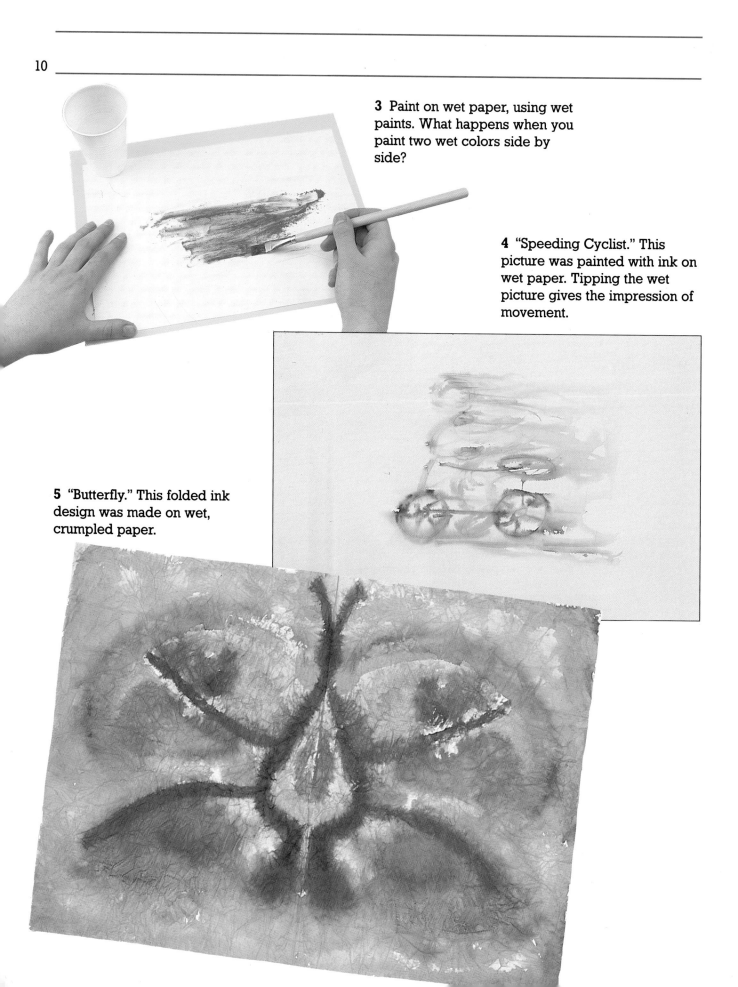

3 Paint on wet paper, using wet paints. What happens when you paint two wet colors side by side?

4 "Speeding Cyclist." This picture was painted with ink on wet paper. Tipping the wet picture gives the impression of movement.

5 "Butterfly." This folded ink design was made on wet, crumpled paper.

A wet circle

A pulling force called surface tension works on the surface of a liquid, which makes it seem as if it has an elastic skin. This keeps it from spreading out over a wider area.

You will need: a sheet of paper, water, a large paintbrush, colored inks, a dropper or a straw.

1 Using a large brush, paint a circle of water on a dry piece of paper. Drop a little colored ink onto the wet circle. Watch the colors blend together and flow out towards the edge of the circle. What happens when the colors reach the edge of the circle? Why do you think this is?

2 "Magic Planet." What happens if you begin with a wet square or a wet triangle?

WATER CAN DILUTE

Water can be added to other liquids to dilute them, that is, to reduce their strength. In art, the strength of water soluble colors, for example, paints, dyes and inks, can be diluted (made weaker) by adding water. The water is the solvent.

Adding water to another liquid dilutes the liquid.

Concentrated fruit drinks need to be diluted with water before you drink them.

Can you think of any other substances that are diluted with water before they are used?

Making a Color Chart

You will need: powder paints, jars or bowls of water, a paintbrush and paper.

1 Add water to some powder paint. Start by making a strong, thick paint, then gradually add water....

.... Make a chart to show how the color changes as you dilute the paint. Notice how the strength of the color becomes weaker and the paint becomes paler in tone.

"A red color chart"

Can you make a chart in reverse by gradually adding more powder color to very dilute watery paint?

Painting with water colors

When you paint with water colors, you do not need to add white paint. The paler colors are made by dilution with water.

"Water color landscape"

WATER EVAPORATES

Water will dry up, or evaporate, in warmth or in a drying wind.

A substance which was dissolved in water is left behind when the water evaporates.

Have you watched laundry blowing in the wind? The water evaporates and the clothes dry quickly.

When you dry your hair with a hair dryer, the warm moving air causes the water to evaporate.

Making salt crystals

You will need: a glass jar (or a pan), a spoon, hot water, salt, thread, a short stick or old pencil, modeling clay, black paper, a light scope or magnifying glass, a pencil and a sheet of white paper.

1 Ask an adult to help you with this part of the experiment. Carefully pour some hot water into the jar or pan. If you use a glass jar, place a spoon in the jar before pouring in the water to prevent the glass from cracking. Once the water is safely in the jar, remove the spoon. Add salt a little at a time, and watch the salt dissolve in the hot water. Continue to add salt until the water has dissolved all the salt it can and some remains at the bottom of the jar. You now have a saturated salt-water solution.

2 Tie a length of thread to the stick or old pencil, then put a little modeling clay on the other end as a weight. Hang the thread in the saturated salt solution for a few days.

3 Watch for salt crystals to form as the water evaporates.

4 Place some of the crystals on the black paper …. and study them through the light scope or magnifying glass. You could also use a microscope to observe your crystals closely. What shape are the crystals?

5 Use a soft drawing pencil to make a sketch of what you see.

6 "Salt crystals – white crayon on black paper."

When water freezes and turns from a liquid into a solid, it becomes snow or ice. Snow is made up of tiny crystals, each of which usually has six sides.

When water is frozen it turns into a solid

Have you tried to catch a snowflake? They melt very quickly in warm hands so are difficult to study closely.

When water turns to ice, it expands. This is why ice is less dense and therefore lighter than water, why ice cubes float in a drink and why icebergs float in the sea.

A snow crystal design

You will need: a small piece of cardboard, a pen or pencil, a ruler, scissors, paper (white and black) and glue.

Like the salt in the last experiment, water in its solid form, snow, is made up of tiny crystals. Each snowflake is a cluster of hexagonal ice crystals.

1 Draw a hexagon on the piece of cardboard, and cut it out.

2 Using the hexagon as a pattern, draw some hexagons on the white paper. You will need about 8.

3 Cut out the hexagons you have drawn.

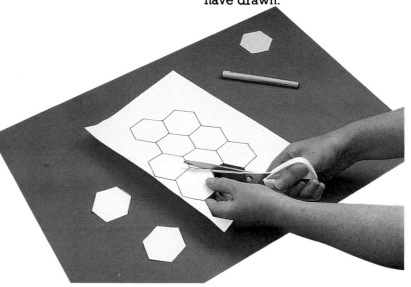

4 Fold each hexagon three times as shown. Cut small pieces from the edges of each folded hexagon.

5 Carefully unfold the cut shapes and glue them onto the black paper to make a snow crystal design.

Like snow crystals, each hexagonal pattern is unique.

Different materials, such as blotting paper, soak up, or absorb, water at different rates.

Some materials absorb water very easily.

After you've washed your hands, you use an absorbent towel to dry them. What might the towel be made of?

Absorbency Test I

You will need: newspaper, a selection of paper types (thick/thin, rough/smooth, shiny/dull), a drinking straw or dropper, water, colored inks, paper clip/tape, a short stick, a bowl, and water-based felt-tip pens.

1 Prepare a selection of small squares from your paper samples.

2 Cover your work surface with a thick layer of newspaper. Using the dropper or straw, drop a blob of water onto the surface of each square. Notice what happens to the blobs. Which papers absorb the water most easily?

Absorbency Test II

1 Choose a paper that absorbs water easily. Drop a spot of colored ink onto the paper and watch it spread. What happens if you drop a second color onto the center of the same spot? Try adding more colors. Watch what happens.

2 Try again, starting with two spots a little bit (6 cm/2½ in) apart. Compare your results.

"Circular design. Inks on blotting paper."

Chromotography

You will need: a very absorbent paper such as a filter paper, paper towel or blotting paper, a short stick, colored inks, water-based felt-tip pens, a bowl and water.

1 Cut pieces of very absorbent paper into strips. Attach the strips to the stick. Make an ink spot on each strip.

2 Pour some water into the bottom of the bowl. Lay the stick across the bowl so that the strips of paper just touch the surface of the water.

3 Watch the water soak along the paper. The water acts as a solvent, carrying the colored ink with it.

Repeat this experiment using different kinds and colors of ink. Try using water-based felt-tip pens, too. Make all your ink spots a similar size, and compare the strips that are produced. What do you notice?

Paper tie-dye

You will need: cold water dyes, water, white paper dinner napkins, and a pair of old rubber gloves.

1 Prepare a small quantity of different colored cold water dyes.

2 Fold a number of white paper dinner napkins in different ways....

Fan folds
Twists
Diagonal folds
Straight folds

3 Dip one end of the folded napkin into a dye. Lift it up quickly so that only a little dye is absorbed. Repeat by dipping the other end, then the middle, into other colors. Leave to dry.

4 Gently unfold the napkin to see the pattern. Do not unfold it before it is dry or it will tear. You can use a warm iron to speed up the drying process.

5 Some interesting tie-dye patterns. Can you tell which pattern was made with a concertina fold?

Materials that do not soak up water at all are waterproof. They resist water. It is possible to make materials which soak up water waterproof, too, by covering them with a coating of wax, oil, or plastic.

When it rains we use umbrellas, raincoats, and boots to keep dry. Have a look at the clothes you wear in the rain. What materials have been used to make them?

Some materials resist water.

These materials are waterproof. They keep water out.

Waterproof Tests

You will need: different types of paper, water, white glue and a paintbrush.

1 Try the absorbency test (see page 17) with squares of plastic, wax paper, aluminum foil and waterproof fabric. How water-resistant are they?

2 Brush some white glue onto a piece of paper and leave to dry. Now brush water over the paper. What do you notice?

Waterproof Pictures

You will need: white glue, paper, paintbrushes, black India ink, colored ink and water.

1 Use diluted white glue to draw a picture on white paper. Leave to dry. Paint an ink wash over the picture. The glue will resist the ink.

2 Draw a picture on a sheet of white paper, using black India ink. Leave to dry.

3 Paint a colored ink wash over the whole picture. The lines already drawn in India ink will resist the ink wash.

WATER AND OIL

Some substances do not dissolve in water. Oil is a good example. It will not mix with water. Instead, oil floats on the surface because it is less dense, or "lighter," than water.

Oil is less dense than water, so it floats on the surface.

Have you seen ducks shaking water from their feathers? The ducks' feathers are oily. How does the oil on their feathers help them to stay afloat?

Sometimes oil is spilled into the sea from a ship. Because oil floats on water, floating booms are used to stop the oil from spreading. It can then be skimmed or pumped from the surface. Detergents can also be used to break down the oil.

Some experiments with oil and water

You will need: a screw-top jar filled with water, and cooking oil.

1 Add a little cooking oil to the water in the jar. Watch what happens.

2 Screw the lid on tightly and shake the jar. What happens?

Patterns with marbling inks

You will need: an old tray, water, marbling inks, drinking straws, paper and liquid detergent.

1 Drop a little of the marbling inks onto the surface of some water in the tray. Why do you think they float on the surface?

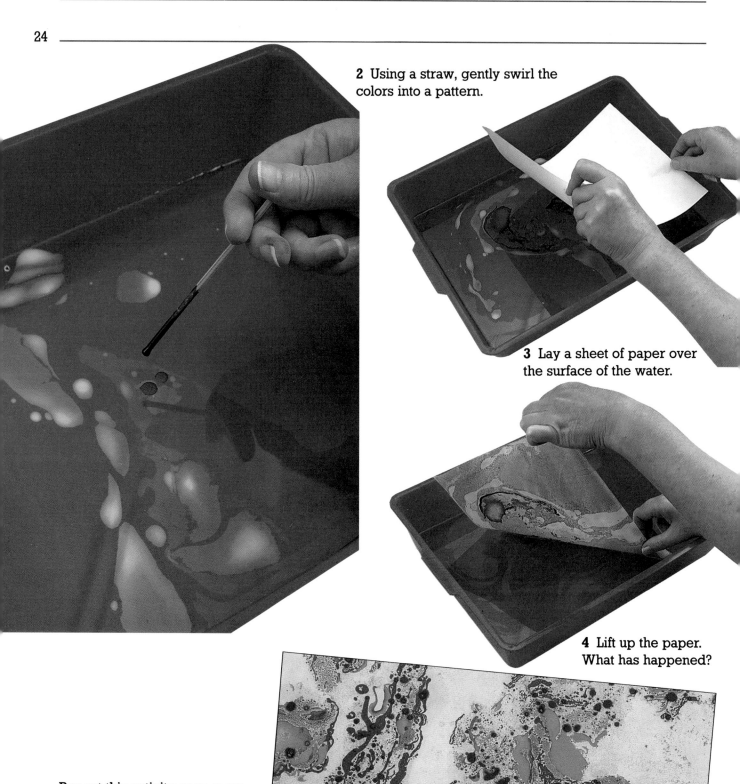

2 Using a straw, gently swirl the colors into a pattern.

3 Lay a sheet of paper over the surface of the water.

4 Lift up the paper. What has happened?

Repeat this activity once more, but this time add a tiny drop of very diluted liquid detergent to the water after you have added the marbling inks. What happens to your design? Can you explain why this is?

An experiment with oil paints and watercolors

You will need: oil paint, linseed oil, watercolor paint, paper, scissors and glue.

1 Dilute some oil paint with a little linseed oil, to make it runny. Drop a little of the diluted oil paint and some watercolor onto a folded sheet of paper.

2 Fold the paper over the colors.... and press gently.

3 Unfold the paper and examine the print. Interesting patterns have been made because the oil paint and watercolors will not mix. Study your patterns. You may find some which remind you of a landscape with water reflections.

4 Cut out some of the patterns and glue them onto a colorful background to make a collage.

If water is pushed, it flows more quickly. Forcing water out of a small hole under pressure creates a powerful jet that travels at high speed. If the hole is very small, the water will be pushed apart and come out in a fine spray. This is called diffusion.

Water forced through a small hole will shoot out in a powerful jet.

Water forced through a very small hole will come out in a spray.

The tiny water droplets in a spray spread out over a wide area.

Have you used a garden hose? You can adjust the nozzle to increase the spread of the water. Can you think of other examples where water is diffused under pressure?

Spray pictures

You will need: a piece of thin cardboard, a pencil, a craft knife, a board (such as a cutting board), a metal ruler, a diffuser spray, colored ink, tape and newspaper.

1 Draw a shape on the piece of thin cardboard. Carefully cut out the shape, using the craft knife.

2 Lift the cut shape out of the cardboard.

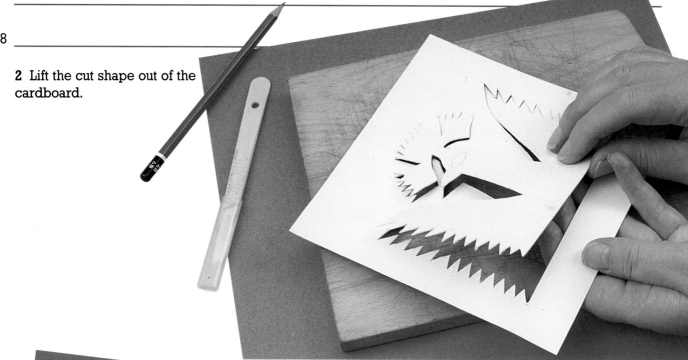

3 Keep the piece of cardboard from which the shape has been cut. This piece of cardboard is a stencil.

4 Tape the cutout shape against a vertical sheet of paper. You will need to protect the background support and floor with newspaper. Using the diffuser, experiment by spraying ink (a water-based liquid) around the edges of the shape.

5 Remove the cardboard shape. What do you notice?

6 Repeat the experiment using the stencil. Spray the ink into the space left by the shape.

7 Compare the two pictures. How do they differ?

Papier-Mâché

Because newspaper is very absorbent, it is a good material to use for papier-mâché.

A glove puppet

1 Mix a small amount of wallpaper paste in a bowl. Tear some newspaper into small pieces and drop them into the paste. Stir well.

2 If the mixture is too stiff, add a little more water.

3 The mixture needs to be stiff enough to mold into a ball shape. This will form the head.

4 Make a tube of thin cardboard to fit over your finger. Push this tube halfway into the head and then shape the features on the puppet's face. When the head is dry, paint the face. Attach the clothes to the tube with white glue.

"Papier-mâché creature"

An illustrated dictionary

Make an illustrated dictionary of words which have links with water, such as water boatman, watercress, waterfall, waterwheel.

A photographic study

Use a camera to take photographs of how water is used in our world. You can begin by using the ideas mentioned in each section of this book.

Painting on fabric

Using watery paints, inks or dyes, paint a picture on a piece of cotton fabric. Watch how the colors are absorbed.

"Three headed monster"

GLOSSARY

Absorb
To soak up. Some materials absorb water easily.

Chromotography
A way of separating different colors.

Crystals
Solids made up of particles called molecules. Molecules are linked together in regular, geometric patterns. Salt crystals are cube shaped, while snow crystals are hexagonal.

Diffusion
Dispersal of liquid in small droplets from one point.

Dilute
To make a solution less strong by adding water.

Dissolve
To break up and become part of a solution. For example, sugar dissolves in water to become a sugar solution.

Dry
Opposite of wet; no moisture.

Evaporation
A drying process in which a liquid becomes a vapor, through heat or drying wind.

Float
To rest on the surface of a liquid; for example, oil will float on water.

Flow
To move easily. The force of gravity will always cause water to flow downward.

Gas
A substance which has no shape. It can fill all the space inside any container.

Liquid
Not a solid, nor a gas, but a runny substance, that can flow. A liquid will take on the shape of any container into which it is poured.

Particle
A tiny piece.

Pressure
A force on a given area.

Resist
To keep out. Materials that resist water do not allow water to be absorbed.

Saturate
To absorb the maximum quantity. A saturated salt-water solution will not allow any more salt to be absorbed.

Solid
A hard shape, not a liquid. A solid keeps its shape.

Solution
Substances — for example, sugar, or salt — can be dissolved in water to make a solution. The water is the solvent.

Solvent
A substance, such as water, which is able to dissolve or form a solution with another substance. Water is a good solvent and is used to make many solutions.

Surface tension
A pulling force on the surface of a liquid, like an invisible elastic skin, which keeps it from spreading out over a wider area.

Water
A colorless, odorless, tasteless liquid. Water is found in all living matter and is necessary for life.

Waterproof
Waterproof materials resist water and keep it from soaking in.

Wet
Opposite of dry; moist with water.